Hueber Lektüren

Ride for Your Life

Pauline O'Carolan

Illustrated by Marjorie Crosby-Fairall

Hueber Verlag

This is the German version of **Ride for Your Life**

Ride for Your Life

ILTS Created and developed by
International Language Teaching Services Limited
Level 1, 1 Market Street
Saffron Walden, Essex CB10 1JB, UK

help@ilts.info
www.ilts.info

Copyright © 2005 International Language Teaching Services Ltd

Author: Pauline O'Carolan
Series editor: James Bean
Illustrations: Marjorie Crosby-Fairall
Text design: ILTS Ltd

| 3. | 2. | 1. | | Die letzten Ziffern |
| 2023 | 22 | 21 | 20 | 19 | bezeichnen Zahl und Jahr des Druckes. |

Alle Drucke dieser Auflage können, da unverändert,
nebeneinander benutzt werden.
1. Auflage
© 2019 Hueber Verlag GmbH & Co. KG, München, Deutschland
Ersetzt die ISBN 978–3–19–202960–8
Redaktion: Heike Birner, Hueber Verlag, München
Umschlaggestaltung: Sieveking · Agentur für Kommunikation, München
Umschlagfoto: © Getty Images/iStock/dotana
Druck und Bindung: Passavia Druckservice GmbH & Co. KG, Passau
Printed in Germany
ISBN 978–3–19–212960–5

Art. 530_26687_001_01

Contents

Chapter 1   A long way from home   4

Chapter 2   A boy and his horse   7

Chapter 3   Where is Aunt Jean?   11

Chapter 4   Lights in the night   15

Chapter 5   A dangerous farm   18

Chapter 6   Riding lessons   21

Chapter 7   Who is in the barn?   26

Chapter 8   Ride for your life   32

Chapter 9   Return to Five Trees Farm   35

Activities   37

Glossary   45

Chapter 1

A long way from home

The bus doors opened. The bus driver looked at the girl. 'Here we are, Miss,' he said. 'Ballycare.'

'Thank you,' said Annie Grant. She looked out of the bus and saw trees and fields of green grass. There was no town. There were no houses and no people.

'Is this it?' Annie asked.

'Yes, Miss,' the bus driver answered. 'It's not a big place. There are some farms and houses.' He showed her a narrow lane. 'If you walk down that lane, you come to a shop. You can ask Mrs Murphy, the shopkeeper, where your friends live.'

'My aunt,' Annie said. 'My mother's sister. I'm going to stay with my Aunt Jean.'

She got off the bus and put her bag on her back. The bus drove away.

Annie wasn't very happy. She was a long way from her home in Scotland. She didn't want to come to Ireland. She liked her Aunt Jean but she really wanted to stay in Glasgow with her mother. But Annie's mother, Sandra, was very sick and had to go into hospital. Sandra didn't have any family in Scotland so she wanted her daughter to go to her sister Jean. Annie and her mother took a bus to the train station in Glasgow. Then Annie took a train to Liverpool in England. There she took a boat at night across the Irish Sea to Dublin. The next morning she took a train from Dublin to Cork.

Aunt Jean wasn't at the train station in Cork to meet Annie. Annie phoned her in Ballycare but she didn't answer. Annie phoned the hospital in Glasgow but she couldn't talk to her mother. Annie waited at the station for a long time. Aunt Jean didn't come. Annie asked at the station about the bus to Ballycare. All the way on the bus she thought, *Where is Aunt Jean? Did she forget me?*

Now it was late in the afternoon. Annie stood on the side of the road. *I must find Mrs Murphy's shop*, she thought. *She'll show me the way to Five Trees Farm.* She looked down the lane. There were hedges on both sides of it. *This way, the driver said.* The sky was getting darker so she walked quickly. She was a city girl and thought the country was dangerous.

Soon she saw the shop at the end of the lane. But she didn't see any people near the shop.

Suddenly she heard a voice calling, 'Jump, Midnight!' A big black horse jumped over a hedge onto the lane in front of her. The horse stopped just before it hit her. On its back was a boy with red hair and green eyes. He was wearing a riding hat.

'You stupid boy!' said Annie. 'Your horse nearly hit me. It's dangerous! And you're a bad rider!'

The boy looked down at Annie. 'I'm not stupid. And Midnight isn't dangerous,' he said. 'We jump over hedges every day and don't hit people.' He smiled a friendly smile. 'I'm Patrick Devlin. My friends call me Pat. I live in Ballycare. Who are you? We don't see many strangers here, little girl.'

'I am a stranger but I'm not a little girl,' Annie said angrily. 'I'm thirteen years old.'

Pat said, 'Thirteen! You're very small. I thought you were ten.'

Annie didn't like this boy. She walked away from him.

'The shop's shut,' he called. 'It shut early today.'

What am I going to do? Annie thought. *I must find Aunt Jean. I must.*

Chapter 2

A boy and his horse

Annie looked back. 'Do you know where Jean Doyle lives?' she asked.

Pat stopped smiling. 'Why do you want to know?'

'My mother is in hospital. She sent me to Ballycare. I'm going to stay with my aunt, Jean Doyle.'

'Your aunt.' Pat's voice wasn't friendly. 'I know Jean Doyle.' He showed Annie a road next to the shop. 'Go that way. Jean Doyle lives five kilometres away. Her farm's called Five Trees Farm.'

'Five kilometres!' said Annie.

'That's not a long way,' Pat said. 'I have to go. I'm late for my dinner.' He looked at her for a minute then rode away down the road to Five Trees Farm.

Annie ran after him and shouted, 'Stupid boy!' But Pat rode very fast and didn't hear her.

Annie walked along the road. She was very tired but she walked on and on.

Then she heard a noise. It was the boy riding Midnight very fast. He stopped in front of Annie.

'I'm sorry,' he said. 'We're friendly people here in Ireland. We like to be kind to strangers. You're in a strange country and your mother's sick in hospital. And I wasn't kind to you.'

'You were very unkind,' Annie said. 'Why?'

Pat's face went red. 'My family and the Doyles…we aren't friends.'

'I'm not a Doyle,' Annie said. 'I don't know very much about Aunt Jean's life in Ireland.'

It was strange. In Aunt Jean's letters to Scotland she talked about her daughter Mary, but she didn't talk about Annie's Uncle Brendan.

'I'm sorry,' said Pat. 'It's a long walk to your aunt's house. Can I take you there on Midnight?'

'Ride on the horse?' Annie asked. She wanted to say no, but Pat was kind to come back.

'Why not?' The boy smiled at her again. He got off the horse and showed her how to get onto Midnight's back. 'Put your foot there.' He helped her get onto the horse.

I'm a long way from the ground, Annie thought.

Pat got on the horse too. 'Come on, Midnight,' he said, and the horse walked along the road.

'What's your name?' Pat asked.

'Annie Grant.'

'You look like your cousin, Mary Doyle,' Pat said. 'She's got long brown hair like you. And big brown eyes.'

'I look like my mother,' Annie said. 'Mum says I look like Aunt Jean too. I don't remember her very well. She visited us in Glasgow when I was six. She was nice – I remember that. But I've never met Mary. Or my uncle.'

Pat rode the horse faster. Annie held on to Pat with her hands and to the horse with her legs. She shut her eyes.

'I don't want to fall off, Pat,' she said.

'You won't fall,' Pat said. 'Riding is fun. Midnight's a very nice animal.'

Annie opened her eyes again and looked at the country around her. It was pretty. There were trees in the fields and flowers in the grass. In Glasgow, Annie lived in a noisy street. There was no grass there and no trees. The only flowers were in shops.

'Look – we're here,' said Pat.

They were at a gate. It was open. Annie saw a white house at the bottom of a small hill. There were trees behind the house. She counted them. One…two…three… four…five. *Five Trees Farm*.

Midnight walked through the gate and down a small road to the house. Annie saw horses in the fields. Pat stopped Midnight next to the house.

'It's very quiet,' Annie said.

'Get down here,' Pat said. 'I must go home now.'

Annie got off Midnight but she didn't want Pat to leave her. It was too quiet. 'Where do you live?' she asked.

'Over the hill, that way,' he said. 'You'll find your aunt now. And your cousin.'

And my Uncle Brendan, she thought.

'Goodbye, Annie Grant,' said Pat.

'Thank you, Pat,' she said. 'I'll see you again.'

He didn't answer but he did smile at her. Then he rode Midnight back to the gate and away down the road. Soon the boy and his horse were gone.

Chapter 3

Where is Aunt Jean?

There were no lights in the windows of the house. Annie knocked at the front door but there was no answer. She knocked louder. She tried to open the door and it opened a little.

She called, 'Hello…Aunt Jean? Are you there? It's Annie.'

The house was quiet. She opened the door wide and walked into the house. She found a light. She was in a long hall with lots of doors. All the doors were shut. She walked to the end of the hall, opened a door and turned on a light. She was in the kitchen. The walls were brown and there were yellow and white curtains over the window. The room had a fireplace but there was no fire in it. There was a big stove with a pot on it. She looked in the pot and saw soup in it. She was very hungry now.

Where is Aunt Jean? Annie thought. *Why isn't she here to meet me?*

She walked back into the hall and opened all the other doors. There was a living room with a television in it. There were three bedrooms. One was her aunt and uncle's room. She saw a picture of her mother on a small table. The second room had a lot of toys in it – Mary's room. Mary was only seven years old. The third room was full of boxes. *Is this my room? There's no bed. Where am I going to sleep?* Annie thought.

The house was empty. But there was soup on the stove, so people were there earlier.

Annie went back into the kitchen. She opened the curtains and looked out the window. She couldn't see any of

the family out there. She was cold so she found a box of matches. *I'll light a fire*, she thought.

She sat on a chair next to the fireplace and watched the fire. She thought about her mother. Was she okay? Annie wanted to phone the hospital. *I'll wait for Aunt Jean to come home*, she thought.

The fire heated the kitchen. It was very quiet for a long time. Annie's eyes shut and she went to sleep. When she woke she heard cars near the house. They stopped. Doors banged. She heard talking. The family was home!

'Wait.' Annie heard her aunt's voice in the hall. 'The lights are on. I didn't turn them on.'

The kitchen door opened. Aunt Jean stood there. Her face was white.

'Oh, Annie! You're here. I'm…I'm so sorry,' she said. 'I couldn't meet you today.'

'That's okay,' Annie said. She didn't understand, but she was happy to see her aunt. 'I came here on the bus.'

Aunt Jean looked behind her then shut the door with a bang. She walked to the fireplace and looked down at Annie.

'Annie, I'll talk to you soon,' she said. 'Stay here for a minute.' She walked quickly out of the room and shut the door behind her.

Annie heard angry men's voices. She heard a man say, 'Get her out of here.' Annie heard Aunt Jean too. Aunt Jean talked very quickly. It was quiet for a minute then Annie heard a car drive away.

Aunt Jean came slowly back into the kitchen. Her hands shook. She looked like Annie's sick mother.

'I'm sorry, Annie,' she said. 'You can't stay here with me. You'll have to go home to Scotland. I must leave Ballycare soon.'

'But, Aunt Jean, I can't go home. Mum's in hospital. You're the only family we have.' Annie had tears in her eyes. 'I'm tired and…and I don't know if Mum is okay.'

Aunt Jean said, 'You can stay here tonight. And you can phone your mother in the hospital tomorrow. It's too late tonight.'

'I want to see Mum,' Annie said, and she cried some more.

Aunt Jean held her for a minute. 'Don't cry, Annie. Perhaps you can stay with a family in the village. Yes, I'll ask tomorrow.' She had tears in her eyes too. 'Are you hungry?' she asked.

'Yes,' Annie said.

Aunt Jean heated the soup on the stove. It was very good. Annie drank two cups of soup then ate some fruit.

'It's time for bed,' Aunt Jean said.

'Where can I sleep?' Annie asked.

'You can sleep in Mary's room tonight.'

They walked down the hall to Mary's room.

'Where is Mary? And where is Uncle Brendan?' Annie asked.

'They're away.'

Aunt Jean said good night quickly and shut the bedroom door. Annie sat on the bed. *What's wrong at Five Trees Farm?* she thought.

Chapter 4

Lights in the night

Annie slept for a long time. She woke at three o'clock in the morning. It was dark and the old house was cold. She turned on a lamp on a table beside the bed. There were some pictures on the table. There was one of Mary with a small white horse, a pony. There was one of Mary when she was younger, with her mother and father. *Will I meet Mary and Uncle Brendan?* thought Annie.

She got out of bed and looked at things in Mary's room. She found a little radio and listened to music quietly. She thought about her mother and Aunt Jean and her family. And she thought about Pat and his horse, Midnight.

Annie opened Mary's curtains and looked out. The moon was high in the black sky. Then she saw lights moving out in the night. *Who's out there?* she thought.

Annie walked quickly to Aunt Jean's room. The door was shut. 'Aunt Jean?' she said.

There was no answer. Annie heard a noise in the room. Quietly she opened the door a little. Aunt Jean was in bed, crying. She cried and cried. She didn't see Annie.

Annie didn't know what to do. She quietly shut the bedroom door. Why was Aunt Jean unhappy? She went back to Mary's room. She looked out the window again. Now there weren't any lights. Annie went back to bed and tried to go back to sleep.

But she couldn't sleep. After an hour she got up, walked through the house and found a coat near the back door. She put it on and went out of the door. She could see easily in the moonlight.

There was a barn behind the house. *Perhaps the lights came from the barn*, Annie thought. The barn was dark now. She walked to the barn, then behind it. There was a white car on the grass. *Is the car's driver in the barn?* she thought. She looked in a window but she couldn't see. It was too dark. She was very quiet and listened carefully. She heard the sound of people sleeping in there.

Annie ran back to the house. Who were these people? Why were they sleeping in the barn? She opened the back door and went into the house.

Aunt Jean was making a cup of tea in the kitchen. She looked very tired and her eyes were red. 'Annie! What is it?' she asked.

'I saw lights in the night so I went to look. There's a car behind the barn and there are people sleeping in the barn,' she said.

Her aunt looked sick. She held Annie's arm. 'Did they see you?' she asked.

'No,' Annie said. 'They were asleep. Who are they?'

'They're farm workers,' Aunt Jean said. 'They sleep in the barn.'

'Oh, okay,' Annie said. Again she didn't understand. Why didn't her uncle do the work on the farm?

'Go back to bed, Annie,' said Aunt Jean. 'I'm tired and I need to sleep.' She carried her cup of tea down the hall to her room. Annie saw the cup shake in her hand.

Annie went back to bed. *I'll ask Aunt Jean some questions in the morning.*

Chapter 5

A dangerous farm

When Annie woke the sun was high in the sky. She dressed and went to find Aunt Jean. Her aunt sat in the kitchen. She was crying again.

'Good morning, Annie. You had a good long sleep,' she said, and tried to smile.

'Are you all right, Aunt Jean?' Annie asked.

'Yes,' her aunt said. 'I'm a little sick today.' She stopped crying, got up and walked to the stove. 'Here's some breakfast,' she said, and she put a plate of eggs on the table.

Annie sat and ate the eggs, and Aunt Jean made her a cup of tea. Annie said, 'Aunt Jean…'

But Aunt Jean said, 'I have to feed the animals,' and left the room.

There was a radio on the mantelpiece above the fireplace. Annie turned the radio on. Music was playing. She listened to it and drank her tea. Then a voice said, 'Good morning. This is the eleven o'clock news. The police are looking for two men who escaped from Cork Prison yesterday.'

Aunt Jean ran into the kitchen and ran over to the mantelpiece. The voice on the radio said, 'The men are dangerous.' Aunt Jean quickly tried to turn off the radio. 'Mick O'Hare and Brendan…' The radio fell off the mantelpiece and broke on the floor.

'Oh dear,' said Aunt Jean.

Annie looked at her. Her aunt didn't want her to hear the news. Why not? Two dangerous men escaped from prison in Cork. There were men in the barn. Were they the same men? Aunt Jean broke the radio before the newsreader said the second name. But Annie thought she knew it. Brendan…*Doyle?* Was Uncle Brendan running away from the police?

'You can phone the hospital in Glasgow now,' Aunt Jean said. Her voice shook. 'And Annie, I'm sorry I didn't meet you yesterday. Please don't tell your mother about it.'

'I won't.'

'Thank you, Annie.'

Annie phoned the hospital and Aunt Jean listened to her. She talked to her mother's doctor. Her mother was all right but Annie couldn't talk to her. She was asleep.

'You can phone again later,' said Aunt Jean.

Annie helped Aunt Jean clean the kitchen. They were both very quiet.

'I'm going out this morning,' said Aunt Jean. 'I have to buy some things at the shops. I'll take the radio with me. And I'll find a place for you to stay in the village.'

'Do I have to stay with strangers?' Annie asked.

'It's the best thing.'

'May I go to the shops with you?'

'No. Stay here, Annie,' she said. 'Please stay in the house. Don't go near the animals. It's dangerous.'

'Why? Aunt Jean, is Uncle Brendan…?'

Aunt Jean said, 'No,' and she took her bag and went quickly out of the room.

Annie heard the front door shut and watched Aunt Jean drive her red car down the road. Then she went into Mary's room. She tried to find Mary's little radio. She wanted to listen to the twelve o'clock news. But she couldn't find it. *Did Aunt Jean take it away too?*

Annie waited for her aunt to return. She opened the front door and looked out. It was a sunny day. She walked out of the house. There were two black horses in a field a long way from the house. Where were the dangerous animals her aunt talked about? There was a pony in a field near the barn. She walked over to it and touched its soft nose. *You're Mary's pony,* she thought. *Uncle Brendan is running away from the police. So where is Mary?*

Chapter 6
Riding lessons

Annie heard a voice calling her. 'Hello there, Annie!' She looked and saw Pat riding on Midnight.

'Pat! Hello.' She was happy to see him. He looked happy to see her too.

'Come for a ride?' he asked.

'Yes, please.'

Pat helped her onto Midnight and they rode away over the fields behind Five Trees Farm.

'Where's your aunt today?' Pat asked.

'She's shopping.' *I'll ask Pat about Uncle Brendan*, she thought. She said, 'Pat…'

But at the same time, Pat said, 'Do you want to learn to ride Midnight?'

'Ride your horse? Yes, please!' Annie was very happy. In Glasgow she rode a skateboard and a bicycle. Her friends at school rode skateboards and bicycles too. She didn't know any horse riders. *I'll ask Pat about Uncle Brendan later*.

Pat stopped Midnight and they both got off her. Then Pat taught Annie how to get on Midnight's back, how to hold the reins and how to make Midnight walk. Annie learnt how to stop Midnight. Pat taught her how to make the horse trot. Annie went up and down. She held the reins tightly at first. She and Midnight did a lot of trotting. It was easy!

'Very good, Annie. I think you'll be a good rider,' Pat said. 'Now I'll teach you to canter.'

'Canter?' she asked.

'That's when a horse runs,' Pat said. 'Cantering is faster than trotting. And galloping is faster than cantering.

Racehorses gallop. But you don't need to gallop.'

'Maybe I don't want to canter,' Annie said.

'You'll be okay,' he said. 'I'll show you.'

Annie got off Midnight. Pat got on the horse's back and said, 'Go, Midnight.' He squeezed her with his legs a little and she trotted. He squeezed her again and said, 'Get up, Midnight,' and Midnight began to canter across the grass. Cantering looked good.

The boy and his horse rode back to Annie. 'Do you want to canter now?' Pat asked.

'Yes.' Annie got on Midnight's back again and squeezed her with her legs. Midnight trotted. Annie squeezed her again and said, 'Get up, Midnight!' Midnight began to canter, but Annie fell off the horse.

'Annie!' Pat called and ran to her. Midnight stopped and ate some grass. Annie lay on her back.

Pat looked down at her. His face was white. 'Annie! Are you okay?'

She smiled up at him. 'I'm okay. It's better than falling off my skateboard in the street. The grass is soft.'

'Perhaps we'll stop our lesson,' Pat said.

'No, Pat, I want to canter today,' Annie said.

'Okay, but put this on.' He gave her his riding hat.

Annie got back on Midnight and squeezed the horse with her legs again. This time she held the reins more tightly and held on to Midnight with her legs. They cantered and cantered.

Pat smiled and called, 'You're a very good rider, Annie.'

Annie rode to some trees at the top of the hill. Then an angry voice said, 'What are you doing on my horse?'

There was a man near her on a brown horse. He rode to her. He had an angry face.

'Your horse?' said Annie. 'This is Pat Devlin's horse, Midnight. Pat's teaching me to ride.'

The man took Midnight's reins. 'I'm William Devlin,' he said. 'And the horse is mine.'

Annie didn't know what to say. They went down the hill to Pat.

'Who is this girl?' Mr Devlin asked.

'Hello, Da,' Pat said. 'Annie's a friend.'

'But who is she?' his father asked.

'I'm Annie Grant.'

Pat's father didn't smile.

Pat said, 'Jean Doyle is Annie's aunt.'

'I don't know why she's your friend, Pat,' said his father. 'A Doyle on our horse!'

Annie was angry. She got off Midnight.

'Annie…' Pat's face was sad.

'Go home, Pat,' his father said.

Pat got on Midnight. 'I'm sorry, Annie,' he said.

Annie walked down the hill, across the fields and back to Five Trees Farm.

Aunt Jean was at the back door. 'Where have you been?' she asked. 'I told you not to go out.'

'I was with Pat Devlin, on a horse called Midnight,' Annie said.

'The Devlins! On their horse!'

'Why not?'

Aunt Jean went into the house.

Annie followed her in. 'Why doesn't Pat's father like your family?' she asked.

'I don't know what you're talking about,' Aunt Jean said angrily.

Where did the happy, kind Aunt Jean go? Annie thought.

Then Annie and her aunt heard some cars arrive. They heard voices. Aunt Jean opened the front door. There were two police cars at the front of the house.

'Mrs Jean Doyle?' a police officer asked.

'Yes,' said Aunt Jean.

'We're looking for Brendan Doyle,' he said.

'He's not here,' Aunt Jean answered. 'You can come in and look for him if you like.'

The police looked for Brendan Doyle and his friend in the house and in the barn. They looked in the fields and behind trees. The men weren't there.

'Have you seen Brendan Doyle?' a police officer asked Annie.

Annie wanted to tell the police about the men in the barn but she saw her aunt's face. She couldn't tell them.

'No,' she said. 'I don't know Brendan Doyle.'

The police left in their cars. Aunt Jean went into the kitchen and shut the door behind her. Annie listened at the door. She heard Aunt Jean speak quietly on the phone. She couldn't hear what her aunt said. When her aunt stopped talking Annie quickly moved away from the door.

It was a long afternoon. Annie lay on Mary's bed and read a book. Then she slept for two hours. At dinner, she and her aunt didn't talk much.

'I've found a family for you to stay with,' Aunt Jean said.

'Okay,' Annie said sadly.

After dinner Annie said, 'I'd like to phone Mum now.' She talked to her mother in hospital. Her mother asked about Aunt Jean, Uncle Brendan and Mary, but Annie didn't say much. She couldn't. She said goodbye to her mother and then went to bed.

I want to go home, she thought.

Chapter 7

Who is in the barn?

Annie heard a car in the night. She thought it was the men coming back but she didn't get up. She didn't sleep well and was very tired in the morning. Aunt Jean was not in the house when Annie got out of bed. There was a letter for her on the kitchen table. It said 'I'M SHOPPING. DON'T GO OUT'.

Shopping again? Annie thought.

She dressed and then ate breakfast. She thought very hard. *Are the men in the barn this morning? Where were they when the police came? And where is Mary?* She walked out of the back door and over to the barn. She saw the white pony in his field. He watched her. The barn door was shut and there was a new lock on the door. Annie walked behind the barn. The white car was not there. Annie tried to look in the barn windows but they were very dirty. She heard a child crying softly in the barn. Was it Mary?

The only way into the barn was through a window. Annie found a rock on the ground and hit one of the windows. There was a loud noise and the glass broke. The child in the barn screamed. Annie looked in. It was dark but she could see Mary in there. She was on the floor. Her hands and legs were tied with rope.

'Mary, it's Annie, your cousin. Don't cry. I'll help you,' Annie called. She tried to take all the broken glass out of the window. She cut her hand.

A voice behind her called, 'Hi, Annie, what are you doing?'

It was Pat. He was riding Midnight down the hill behind the barn.

'Pat, come here quickly,' Annie said. 'Mary's in the barn. She's tied with rope. I'm trying to get in the window but I cut my hand.'

Pat jumped off Midnight and tied her to a tree near the barn. He looked into the barn and saw Mary.

'I'm going to get in the window. I'll get Mary out,' he said.

Pat got in the window. Mary stopped crying. He picked up the little girl and carried her to the window.

'She's easy to carry,' Pat said. 'She's very light.'

He gave Mary to Annie. Annie put her on the grass. Pat got out of the window then untied Mary's ropes. Mary stood up. She tried to walk. 'My legs hurt,' she said.

'Sit down, Mary,' Pat said.

'Where's Mummy?' Mary asked.

'She's shopping,' Annie said. 'She'll be home soon. Who did this to you, Mary?'

'The man with Daddy,' said Mary. 'I don't like him. He tied me up.'

'Come over here,' Pat said to Annie. They moved away from Mary. Pat spoke quietly. 'This is bad, Annie,' he said. 'Your uncle's escaped from prison. You know that, don't you?'

'Yes,' said Annie. 'With another man.'

Pat said, 'Two men robbed a shop in Mallow this morning. The police think your uncle did it. The radio news said a woman was there too. Your aunt…'

'Aunt Jean isn't a robber,' Annie said angrily.

'No,' Pat said. 'But maybe your uncle is making her help him. Maybe that's why they took Mary. Brendan Doyle is a bad man. And the other man – Mick O'Hare – is worse. He's dangerous.'

'My mother and I didn't know Uncle Brendan was in prison. Aunt Jean didn't tell us,' Annie said.

Mary came over to them. 'Mummy was too sad,' she said. 'Daddy stole horses from other farmers and sold them.'

Annie looked at Pat. 'Did he steal your father's horses, Pat?'

'Yes,' he said. 'My father was away in England. One day Brendan Doyle stole my father's best horses. Later the police caught him stealing horses from another farmer in Ballycare. Doyle didn't tell the police where he put my father's horses. The horses didn't have any food and they died.'

Annie was very sad. 'Those poor horses.'

'We have to phone the police,' said Pat. 'Come on.'

'Will we take Daddy's money with us?' asked Mary.

'What money?' said Pat.

Mary said, 'Daddy put his money in a hole in the barn.'

'Where?' Annie asked.

'In the floor,' she said. 'Look!' She walked to the barn window. Annie and Pat followed her and looked in the window. 'Over there,' Mary said. 'It's in the corner under the floor.'

Pat said, 'I'll go back in and look.' He got in the window and went to the corner. He looked at the floor and found the hole under it. He took out a black backpack, carried it to the window and gave it to Annie.

Annie opened the backpack. It was full of money.

Pat said, 'The police didn't find Brendan Doyle's money when he went to prison.'

Mary said, 'Daddy and the other man took me with them in their car yesterday. He went to find his horse money.'

'I think this is it. We'll take the money to the police,' Annie said. She shut the backpack and put it on her back. 'We can phone from the house. Hurry! The men will be back.'

Pat carried Mary on his back. But the young people were too late. Two cars were driving up the road. One was Aunt Jean's red car. The other car was the white one that Annie saw behind the barn.

'It's them!' Annie called. 'They'll see the backpack.'

The cars stopped at the house.

Pat said, 'Quick. Run back to Midnight, Annie. Ride to Mrs Murphy's shop. Fast! Phone the police from there. I'll take Mary on the pony and ride to my house. My father is home. He'll help us.'

Pat took Mary to the white pony and put her on it. He got onto the pony's back and called, 'Go, Annie! Midnight's a fast horse. Ride for your life!'

Chapter 8

Ride for your life

Pat and Mary rode away across the fields. Annie ran back to Midnight. She untied her from the tree and got on her back. 'Go, Midnight,' she said and squeezed her with her legs. The horse walked. Annie squeezed her harder.

'Go, Midnight, go,' she said.

Suddenly a man ran out from behind the barn. Annie knew his face from the photo in Mary's room. It was Brendan Doyle. 'Stop!' he called. 'Get off that horse!' He jumped at Midnight and tried to get Annie off the horse.

Midnight kicked Doyle and he fell onto the ground. Midnight trotted very fast. Annie looked behind her. Doyle was getting up. His leg was hurt. He saw the black backpack and screamed, 'That's my bag! Give me my money!'

Annie squeezed Midnight and the horse cantered. Near the house, Annie saw the other man with her aunt. He was holding her arms and she was crying. Annie couldn't stop to help her, but she rode Midnight at the man. He jumped back and Aunt Jean escaped from him. She ran to her red car.

Annie heard Doyle shout, 'Leave her, Mick. The girl's got our money. Get in the car.'

Midnight was cantering very fast. Annie held the reins tightly and almost lay down on Midnight's back.

She heard cars and looked behind her. Aunt Jean was driving her red car in front of the white car. Then the white car moved beside the red one and hit it. The red one stopped at the side of the road. Annie hoped Aunt Jean was okay. Now the white car was coming closer to her.

She rode Midnight down the road. Soon they were near the shop. 'Help! Help!' Annie shouted.

Mrs Murphy came out of the shop.

'Help me, please,' Annie called to her. 'Brendan Doyle is in that car. Phone the police. And lock your door – he's dangerous!'

Mrs Murphy ran back into the shop.

'Go faster, Midnight,' Annie said, and Midnight galloped. They rode and rode. Then Midnight slowed. She was tired. The car came closer. Annie looked behind her. One of the men put his arm out of the car window. There was a small black gun in his hand. Annie heard a loud noise. *He's firing the gun at us!* she thought.

Annie saw a gate in a hedge beside the road. She made Midnight canter to the gate. 'Jump, Midnight!' Midnight jumped high over the gate and came down on the soft grass. Midnight's back was wet and her legs shook.

Then there was a loud noise behind them. *What was that?* thought Annie. *The car...What did it hit?*

The noise made Midnight canter again. Annie didn't look behind her.

Chapter 9

Return to Five Trees Farm

Midnight cantered across the fields with Annie on her back. Then she slowed, and they walked for a long time. At last there were houses in front of them. They came to a road. Then Annie heard a car behind them.

Is it the men? thought Annie.

But it was not the white car. It was a green one. It stopped next to them. Pat and his father were in it. And Aunt Jean and Mary were in the back. They all got out of the car.

'We found your aunt near Five Trees Farm,' Pat said.

Aunt Jean's arm was hurt. But she held Annie tightly with her other arm. 'Annie, Annie, you're okay!'

Pat said, 'The police found Brendan Doyle and his friend. Their car hit a tree.'

Annie looked at Aunt Jean and Mary. Their eyes were red.

'Is Uncle Brendan okay?' she asked.

Pat said quietly, 'The men are badly hurt.'

'I'm sorry, Aunt Jean,' Annie said.

'Thank you, Annie.' Aunt Jean tried to smile. 'Brendan will be okay. He'll go back to prison later, but he'll be okay.'

Pat's father said, 'Hello, Annie.' He shook her hand. 'I want to say sorry. I wasn't very nice to you, was I? You and your aunt and cousin didn't steal my horses.'

'You were angry about your horses. I understand,' she said.

'My father says you're a very good rider, Annie,' Pat said.

'Midnight is the best horse. But she's very tired after that ride,' Annie said.

Mr Devlin smiled. 'She can stay with a friend of mine here in town. We'll take her home tomorrow.'

Aunt Jean said, 'We'll take you to see the police now, Annie. Then we can go home too.'

Annie asked, 'What about you, Aunt Jean? Did you help Uncle Brendan? Will you go to prison too?'

Aunt Jean said, 'Brendan escaped from prison. He phoned me. He wanted to see Mary. Mary loves her father so we went to see him. Mick O'Hare was with Brendan and he took Mary. Then I had to help them.'

'The police know why your aunt helped them,' said Mr Devlin. 'She'll be okay.'

Annie was very happy to hear that. 'And can I stay at Five Trees Farm now?'

'Of course,' said Aunt Jean and smiled.

Annie talked to the police, and then Mr Devlin drove her and the others back to the farm. Annie slept for hours in Mary's bed. She hurt all over.

'I may be a good horse rider but I'm a very new rider,' she said to her aunt later.

That night Aunt Jean cooked a big meal and Pat and his father came to visit. They all had a good time. Aunt Jean and Mary looked happier.

The phone rang. Aunt Jean answered it. She talked for a minute then said, 'It's for you, Annie.'

It was Annie's mother. She was phoning from Glasgow. She was much better.

'Are you having a good time with Aunt Jean?' she asked.

'I'm having a very good time,' Annie said. 'I can ride a horse now.' She didn't tell her mother about her ride that day.

Aunt Jean smiled at her. The real story of Annie's visit to Ballycare could wait.

Activities

Chapters 1 and 2

Before you read

A. Look at the picture on page 6 and circle the correct answers.
1. What is the girl carrying?
   a. a book   b. a hat   c. a bag
2. How does the girl look?
   a. angry   b. happy   c. sad

B. Find these words in your dictionary. Use them in the sentences.

   hospital   dangerous   stranger   hedge

1. We have a _____ around our garden.
2. I've never seen him before. He's a _____ in this town.
3. Jill had to go to _____ after her car accident.
4. It's _____ to drive and talk on a mobile phone.

C. Listen to Track 3 on the CD and answer these questions.
1. Who is speaking?
   a. a girl and a woman   b. a boy and a man   c. a girl and a man
2. Where are they?
   a. on a bus   b. in a car   c. in a shop
3. What are they talking about?
   a. shopping   b. where the girl needs to go   c. the weather

After you read

COMPREHENSION

A. Circle the correct answers.
1. Why did Annie want to stay in Glasgow?
   a. Because she was sick.   b. Because she didn't like Ireland.
   c. Because she wanted to be with her mother.
2. What was Pat's family name?
   a. Grant   b. Doyle   c. Devlin
3. Why did Pat ride back to Annie?
   a. to tell her his name   b. to say sorry and be kind to her
   c. to ask her how old she was
4. Where did Pat take Annie?
   a. to her aunt's house   b. to the shop   c. to the train station

B. Circle T for true or F for false for these sentences.
1. The horse hit Annie when it jumped over the hedge.   T / F
2. At first, Annie liked Pat.   T / F
3. The shop was open when Annie got there.   T / F
4. Pat's family and Aunt Jean's family were good friends.   T / F

C. Complete these sentences.
1. Annie's mother was sick and had to go into _____.
2. Annie didn't see any people near the _____.
3. In her letters, Aunt Jean didn't talk about Annie's Uncle
_____.
4. There were five trees behind the _____.

D. Write short answers to these questions.
1. What was the shopkeeper's name?
_____
2. How far was Aunt Jean's farm from the shop?
_____
3. What was Aunt Jean's farm called?
_____
4. Who did Pat tell Annie she looked like?
_____

LANGUAGE ACTIVITIES

A. Write the correct prepositions in the spaces.

of   about   in   at

1. The bus driver looked _____ Annie.
2. Annie stood on the side _____ the road.
3. In her letters, Aunt Jean talked _____ her daughter
   Mary.
4. There were trees _____ the fields.

B. Write the missing letters to make words from Chapters 1 and 2.
1. h _ dg _ s   3. fl _ w _ rs
2. tr _ _ s   4. gr _ ss

WHAT DO YOU THINK?
Listen to Chapters 1 and 2 on the CD. Do you think Aunt Jean will
be there to welcome Annie to Five Trees Farm? Why or why not?

Chapters 3, 4 and 5

Before you read

A. Answer these questions about the story so far.
1. What time of day was it when Annie arrived at the house?
   a. the morning   b. the middle of the day   c. the evening
2. Who did Annie expect to see at the house?
   a. Aunt Jean and her family   b. her mother
   c. Pat and his family

B. Find these words in your dictionary. Use them in the sentences.

curtains   knock   barn   shake

1. Please _____ on the door before you come into my room.
2. When the train goes past it makes the house _____.
3. Close the _____ so nobody can look in the window.
4. The animals are kept in the _____ at night.

C. Listen to Track 4 on the CD and answer these questions.
1. Who answers when Annie calls out?
   a. Aunt Jean   b. nobody
2. Is Annie able to get into the house?
   a. yes   b. no
3. How does Annie feel?
   a. hungry and a little worried   b. hungry but happy

After you read

COMPREHENSION
A. Circle the correct answers.
1. What was on the stove?
   a. a fire   b. a kettle   c. a pot of soup
2. Who did Annie hear talking angrily to Aunt Jean after she walked out of the kitchen?
   a. children   b. men   c. women
3. What was the radio news story about?
   a. Annie's mother   b. two dangerous men   c. two children
4. What happened to the radio when it fell off the mantelpiece?
   a. It got louder.   b. It broke.   c. Annie turned it on.

B. Circle T for true or F for false for these sentences.
1. Aunt Jean looked happy to see Annie.   T / F
2. Aunt Jean said Annie could stay as long as she liked.   T / F
3. Annie heard people sleeping in the barn.   T / F
4. Aunt Jean said Annie could go shopping with her.   T / F

C. Complete these sentences.
1. Aunt Jean looked like Annie's sick _____.
2. Aunt Jean thought Annie could stay with a family in the _____.
3. Annie woke at three o'clock in the _____.
4. There was a pony in the field near the _____.

D. Write short answers to these questions.
1. Who did Annie see in the pictures beside Mary's bed?
   _____
2. What was Aunt Jean doing in bed when Annie looked in her room?
   _____
3. Who did Aunt Jean say was sleeping in the barn?
   _____
4. Who did Annie think her uncle was running away from?
   _____

LANGUAGE ACTIVITIES
A. Match these words to make words from Chapters 3, 4 and 5.
1. bed   reader
2. moon   place
3. fire   room
4. news   light

B. Write the missing letters to make words from Chapters 3, 4 and 5.
1. st _ v _   3. m _ tch _ s
2. f _ r _   4. m _ nt _ lp _ _ c _

WHAT DO YOU THINK?
Listen to Chapters 3, 4 and 5 on the CD. Who do you think was sleeping in the barn?

Chapters 6 and 7

Before you read

A. *Look at the picture on page 23 and circle the correct answers.*
1. Who is riding Midnight?
   a. Annie   b. Pat   c. Aunt Jean
2. How does the man on the other horse look?
   a. friendly   b. angry   c. sad

B. *Find these words in your dictionary. Use them in the sentences.*

   reins   gallop   escaped   backpack

1. He was a good rider. He could make the horse _____very fast.
2. I put my schoolbooks in my _____ and left the house.
3. To control the horse, pull on the _____.
4. Luckily, the family _____ from the burning house.

C. *Listen to Track 5 on the CD and answer these questions.*
1. Who is speaking?
   a. a boy and a girl   b. a man and a girl
2. How do they feel?
   a. angry   b. happy
3. Who does Annie want to ask Pat about?
   a. Aunt Jean   b. Uncle Brendan

After you read

COMPREHENSION

A. *Circle the correct answers.*
1. What was the first thing Pat taught Annie how to do?
   a. get on the horse   b. make the horse trot
   c. make the horse canter
2. Who was the owner of Midnight?
   a. Pat   b. William Devlin   c. Jean Doyle
3. What did Annie tell the police about Brendan Doyle?
   a. He was in the barn.   b. He was dangerous.
   c. She didn't know him.
4. Who did Annie find in the barn?
   a. Pat's dad   b. her cousin Mary   c. Uncle Brendan

B. Circle T for true or F for false for these sentences.
1. Pat said Annie was a bad rider.   T / F
2. The police wanted to know where Uncle Brendan was. T / F
3. Pat's father stole Uncle Brendan's horses and they died. T / F
4. Pat told Annie to ride Midnight to Mrs Murphy's shop. T / F

C. Complete these sentences.
1. Annie wasn't hurt when she fell because the grass was
   _____.
2. The police looked for the men in the house and in the
   _____.
3. Mary's hands and legs were tied with _____.
4. The police didn't find Brendan Doyle's money when he went to
   _____.

D. Write short answers to these questions.
1. What happened to Annie the first time Midnight cantered?
   _____
2. What did the letter on the kitchen table say?
   _____
3. What was in the black backpack?
   _____
4. Who owned the red car?
   _____

LANGUAGE ACTIVITIES
A. Circle the correct verb forms in these sentences.
1. The man said, 'What are you **do** / **doing** / **done** on my horse?'
2. Annie wanted **tell** / **to tell** / **told** the police about the men.
3. Two men **robbed** / **to rob** / **robbing** a shop this morning.
4. Pat **speak** / **spoke** / **speaking** quietly.

B. Write the missing letters to make words from Chapters 6 and 7.
1. sq _ _ _ z _ d   3. scr _ _ m _ d
2. sm _ l _ d   4. st _ l _

WHAT DO YOU THINK?
Listen to Chapters 6 and 7 on the CD. Do you think Aunt Jean has been helping Brendan Doyle and Mick O'Hare? Why or why not?

Chapters 8 and 9

Before you read

A. Look at the picture on page 33 and circle the correct answers.
1. Who do you think the woman standing outside the shop is?
   a. Aunt Jean   b. Mrs Murphy   c. Annie's mother
2. How do you think Annie feels?
   a. scared   b. happy   c. bored

B. Find these words in your dictionary. Use them in the sentences.

   screamed   firing   tightly   hurt

1. I held the dog _____ so it couldn't run away.
2. What's that noise? Is someone _____ a gun?
3. John's leg was _____ when he fell off his bike.
4. The children _____ for help and the fire fighter went and saved them.

C. Listen to Track 6 on the CD and answer these questions.
1. What did Annie say to Midnight?
   a. 'Go, Midnight.'   b. 'Stop, Midnight.'
2. What happened to Brendan Doyle's leg?
   a. It was hot.   b. It was hurt.
3. Did Annie speak to Brendan Doyle?
   a. yes   b. no

After you read

COMPREHENSION

A. Circle the correct answers.
1. Who did Midnight kick?
   a. Annie   b. Aunt Jean   c. Brendan Doyle
2. What did Annie make Midnight jump over?
   a. the white car   b. a gate   c. the red car
3. What happened to Brendan Doyle and Mick O'Hare?
   a. They were badly hurt.   b. They escaped.
   c. They were killed.
4. Why had Aunt Jean helped Brendan Doyle and Mick O'Hare?
   a. Because she loved Brendan.   b. Because she hated the police.
   c. Because Mick O'Hare had taken Mary.

B. Circle T for true or F for false for these sentences.
1. Aunt Jean tried to kill Annie.   T / F
2. Midnight got tired while Annie was riding her.   T / F
3. Pat's father said sorry to Annie.   T / F
4. Annie told her mother about Uncle Brendan later that day. T / F

C. Complete these sentences.
1. Annie told Mrs Murphy to phone the _____.
2. After jumping over the gate, Midnight's back was _____.
3. The men's car hit a _____.
4. When she phoned, Annie's mother was much _____.

D. Write short answers to these questions.
1. Who was in the white car?
   _____

2. Who came out of the shop when Annie rode past?
   _____

3. Who was in the green car?
   _____

4. What did Annie tell her mother that she could do now?
   _____

LANGUAGE ACTIVITIES
A. Write the correct prepositions in the spaces.

   on behind at across

1. Pat and Mary rode away _____ the fields.
2. Annie almost lay down _____ Midnight's back.
3. Annie heard a car _____ them.
4. Aunt Jean smiled _____ Annie.

B. Write the past tense of these verbs.
1. ride _____   3. hear _____
2. ring _____   4. drive _____

WHAT DO YOU THINK?
Listen to Chapters 8 and 9 on the CD. How do you think Aunt
Jean felt when the men made her help them?

_____

Do you think Annie will enjoy her stay at Five Trees Farm now?

_____

Glossary

adj. adjective; *adv.* adverb; *n.* noun; *v.* verb

backpack /ˈbækˌpæk/ *n.*	Rucksack
bang /bæŋ/ *v.*	Knall
n.	zuschlagen
barn /bɑːn/ *n.*	Scheune
cousin /ˈkʌzn/ *n.*	Cousin/Cousine
curtain /ˈkɜːtn/ *n.*	Vorhang
escape /ɪˈskeɪp/ *v.*	ausbrechen, flüchten
fall /fɔːl/ *v.*	(herunter)fallen
fireplace /ˈfaɪəˌpleɪs/ *n.*	Kamin
gallop /ˈgæləp/ *v.*	galoppieren
gate /geɪt/ *n.*	Tor
hall /hɔːl/ *n.*	Flur
hedge /hedʒ/ *n.*	Hecke
hospital /ˈhɒspɪtl/ *n.*	Krankenhaus
knock /nɒk/ *v.*	klopfen
lane /leɪn/ *n.*	Weg, Feldweg
lock /lɒk/ *n.*	Schloss
v.	abschließen
mantelpiece /ˈmæntlˌpiːs/ *n.*	Kaminsims
news /njuːz/ *n.*	Nachrichtensendung
newsreader /ˈnjuːzˌriːdə/ *n.*	Nachrichtensprecher(in)
pony /ˈpəʊni/ *n.*	Pony
prison /ˈprɪzn/ *n.*	Gefängnis
rein /reɪn/ *n.*	Zügel
rob /rɒb/ *v.*	(aus)rauben
rope /rəʊp/ *n.*	Seil, Strick
shake /ʃeɪk/ *v.*	schütteln
shook /ʃʊk/ *v.*	schüttelte (*past tense* von *shake*)
skateboard /ˈskeɪtˌbɔːd/ *n.*	Skateboard

soup /suːp/ *n.*	Suppe
steal /stiːl/ *v.*	stehlen
stole /stəʊl/ *v.*	stahl (*past tense* von *steal*)
stove /stəʊv/ *n.*	Ofen, Herd
stranger /ˈstreɪndʒə/ *n.*	Fremde(r)
stupid /ˈstjuːpɪd/ *adj.*	dumm
tear /tɪə/ *n.*	Träne
tie /taɪ/ *v.*	fesseln
tightly /ˈtaɪtli/ *adv.*	fest
trot /trɒt/ *v.*	traben
untie /ʌnˈtaɪ/ *v.*	losbinden, entfesseln
woke /wəʊk/ *v.*	wachte auf (*past tense* von *wake*)

Ride for Your Life
Activities: Answer Key

Chapters 1 and 2
Before you read
A. 1. c, 2. a   B. 1. hedge, 2. stranger, 3. hospital, 4. dangerous   C. 1. c, 2. a, 3. b

After you read
Comprehension
A. 1. c, 2. c, 3. b, 4. a   B. 1. F, 2. F, 3. F, 4. F   C. 1. hospital, 2. shop, 3. Brendan, 4. house

D. 1. Mrs Murphy, 2. five kilometres, 3. Five Trees Farm, 4. her cousin, Mary Doyle

Language activities
A. 1. at, 2. of, 3. about, 4. in   B. 1. hedges, 2. trees, 3. flowers, 4. grass

What do you think?
Student's own answers

Chapters 3, 4 and 5
Before you read
A. 1. c, 2. a   B. 1. knock, 2. shake, 3. curtains, 4. barn   C. 1. b, 2. a, 3. a

After you read
Comprehension
A. 1. c, 2. b, 3. b, 4. b   B. 1. F, 2. F, 3. T, 4. F   C. 1. mother, 2. village, 3. morning, 4. barn

D. 1. Mary, Mary's mother and Mary's father, 2. crying, 3. farm workers, 4. the police

Language activities
A. 1. bedroom, 2. moonlight, 3. fireplace, 4. newsreader

B. 1. stove, 2. fire, 3. matches, 4. mantelpiece

What do you think?
Students' own answers

Chapters 6 and 7
Before you read
A. 1. a, 2. b   B. 1. gallop, 2. backpack, 3. reins, 4. escaped   C. 1. a, 2. b, 3. b

After you read
Comprehension
A. 1. a, 2. b, 3. c, 4. b   B. 1. F, 2. T, 3. F, 4. T   C. 1. soft, 2. barn, 3. rope, 4. prison

D. 1. She fell off the horse. 2. I'M SHOPPING. DON'T GO OUT. 3. money, 4. Aunt Jean

Language activities
A. 1. doing, 2. to tell, 3. robbed, 4. spoke   B. 1. squeezed, 2. smiled, 3. screamed, 4. stole

What do you think?
Students' own answers

Chapter 8 and 9
Before you read
A. 1. b, 2. a   B. 1. tightly, 2. firing, 3. hurt, 4. screamed   C. 1. a, 2. b, 3. b

After you read
Comprehension
A. 1. c, 2. b, 3. a, 4. c   B. 1. F, 2. T, 3. T, 4. F   C. 1. police, 2. wet, 3. tree, 4. better

D. 1. Brendan Doyle and Mick O'Hare, 2. Mrs Murphy, 3. Pat, his father (Mr Devlin), Aunt Jean and Mary, 4. ride a horse

Language activities
A. 1. across, 2. on, 3. behind, 4. at   B. 1. rode, 2. rang, 3. heard, 4. drove

What do you think?
Students' own answers